EMG3-0143
合唱楽譜＜スタンダード＞

STANDARD CHORUS PIECE

合唱で歌いたい！スタンダードコーラスピース

混声3部合唱

YOU RAISE ME UP (English ver.)

作詞：Brendan Joseph Graham　　作曲：Rolf Lovland　　合唱編曲：奥田悌三

●●● 曲目解説 ●●●

アイルランド／ノルウェーのミュージシャン、シークレット・ガーデンが2002年に発表した楽曲です。アイルランド民謡『ロンドンデリーの歌』（『ダニー・ボーイ』）の旋律を元に作られました。ヴァイオリンで静かに始まるどこか切ない旋律と、深い信仰と確たる愛を感じる「主」への祈りが込められた歌詞。そして、優美で壮大なクライマックスを飾るこの一曲は、CMやドラマの挿入歌に起用されるほか、結婚式でも定番の曲となり、さまざまなシーンで人々の心に深い感動を残す楽曲となりました。天に響き渡るようなハーモニーで感動に包まれる音楽を奏でてみてはいかがでしょうか。

【この楽譜は、旧商品『YOU RAISE ME UP（English Ver.）（混声3部合唱）』（品番：EME-C3017）とアレンジ内容に変更はありません。】

合唱で歌いたい！スタンダードコーラス

YOU RAISE ME UP (English ver.)

作詞：Brendan Joseph Graham　作曲：Rolf Lovland　合唱編曲：奥田悌三

YOU RAISE ME UP
Words by Brendan Joseph Graham　Music by Rolf Lovland
© Copyright ALFRED MUSIC PUBLISHING CO., INC
All rights reserved. Used by permission.　Print rights for Japan administered by Yamaha Music Entertainment Holdings, Inc.
© PEERMUSIC (UK) LTD.　International copyright secured. All rights reserved.　Rights for Japan administered by PEERMUSIC K.K.

Elevato Music
EMG3-0143

YOU RAISE ME UP (English ver.)

作詞:Brendan Joseph Graham

When I am down and oh my soul so weary
When troubles come and my heart burdened be
Then I am still and wait here in the silence
Until you come and sit a while with me

You raise me up so I can stand on mountains
You raise me up to walk on stormy seas
I am strong when I am on your shoulders
You raise me up to more than I can be

There is no life - no life without its hunger
Each restless heart beats so imperfectly
But when you come and I am filled with wonder
Sometimes I think I glimpse eternity

You raise me up so I can stand on mountains
You raise me up to walk on stormy seas
I am strong when I am on your shoulders
You raise me up to more than I can be

You raise me up so I can stand on mountains
You raise me up to walk on stormy seas
I am strong when I am on your shoulders
You raise me up to more than I can be

You raise me up to more than I can be

エレヴァートミュージックエンターテイメントはウィンズスコアが
展開する「合唱楽譜・器楽系楽譜」を中心とした専門レーベルです。

ご注文について

エレヴァートミュージックエンターテイメントの商品は全国の楽器店、ならびに書店にてお求めになれますが、店頭でのご購入が困難な場合、下記PC&モバイルサイト・FAX・電話からのご注文で、直接ご購入が可能です。

◎PCサイト&モバイルサイトでのご注文方法

http://elevato-music.com

上記のアドレスへアクセスし、WEBショップにてご注文ください。

◎FAXでのご注文方法

FAX.03-6809-0594

24時間、ご注文を承ります。上記PCサイトよりFAXご注文用紙をダウンロードし、印刷、ご記入の上ご送信ください。

◎お電話でのご注文方法

TEL.0120-713-771

営業時間内に電話いただければ、電話にてご注文を承ります。

※この出版物の全部または一部を権利者に無断で複製(コピー)することは、著作権の侵害にあたり、著作権法により罰せられます。

※造本には十分注意しておりますが、万一、落丁・乱丁などの不良品がありましたらお取り替えいたします。また、ご意見・ご感想もホームページより受け付けておりますので、お気軽にお問い合わせください。